The Passionate
State of Mind

Also by Eric Hoffer

❄

The True Believer

Eric Hoffer

The Passionate State of Mind

~

and other aphorisms

Buccaneer Books
Cutchogue, New York

International Standard Book Number: 1-56849-032-1

For ordering information, contact:

Buccaneer Books, Inc.
P.O. Box 168
Cutchogue, N.Y. 11935

(516) 734-5724, Fax (516) 734-7920

To

ELIZABETH LAWRENCE

The Passionate
State of Mind

1

THERE is in most passions a shrinking away from ourselves. The passionate pursuer has all the earmarks of a fugitive.

Passions usually have their roots in that which is blemished, crippled, incomplete and insecure within us. The passionate attitude is less a response to stimuli from without than an emanation of an inner dissatisfaction.

2

A POIGNANT dissatisfaction, whatever be its cause, is at bottom a dissatisfaction with ourselves. It is surprising how much hardship and humiliation a man will endure without bitterness when he has not the least doubt about his worth or when he is so integrated with others that he is not aware of a separate self.

3

THAT we pursue something passionately does not always mean that we really want it or have a special aptitude for it. Often, the thing we pursue most passionately is but a substitute for the one thing we really want and cannot have. It is usually safe to predict that the fulfillment of an excessively cherished desire is not likely to still our nagging anxiety.

In every passionate pursuit, the pursuit counts more than the object pursued.

4

IT SEEMS that we are most busy when we do not do the one thing we ought to do; most greedy when we cannot have the one thing we really want; most hurried when we can never arrive; most self-righteous when irrevocably in the wrong.

There is apparently a link between excess and unattainability.

5

IT IS strange how the moment we have reason to be dissatisfied with ourselves we are set upon by a pack of insistent clamorous desires. Is desire somehow an expression of the centrifugal force that tears and pulls us away from an undesirable self? A gain in self-esteem usually reduces the pull of the appetites, while a crisis in self-esteem is likely to cause a weakening or a complete breakdown of self-discipline.

Asceticism is sometimes a deliberate effort to reverse a reaction in the chemistry of our soul: by suppressing desire we try to rebuild and bolster self-esteem.

6

TO BELIEVE that if we could but have this or that we would be happy is to suppress the realization that the cause of our unhappiness is in our inadequate and blemished selves. Excessive desire is thus a means of suppressing our sense of worthlessness.

7

EVERY intense desire is perhaps basically a desire to be different from what we are. Hence probably the imperiousness of the desire for fame, which is a desire for a self utterly unlike the real self.

8

THERE is even in the most selfish passion a large element of self-abnegation. It is startling to realize that what we call extreme self-seeking is actually self-renunciation. The miser, health addict, glory chaser and their like are not far behind the selfless in the exercise of self-sacrifice.

Every extreme attitude is a flight from the self.

9

DISSIPATION is a form of self-sacrifice. The reckless wasting of one's vigor is a blind striving to "liquidate" an unwanted self. And as one would expect, the passage from this to other forms of self-sacrifice is not uncommon. Passionate sinning has not infrequently been an apprenticeship to sainthood. Many of the insights of the saint stem from his experience as a sinner.

10

THE dislocation involved in switching from one passion to another—even its very opposite—is less than one would expect. There is a basic similarity in the make-up of all passionate minds. The sinner who turns saint undergoes no more drastic transformation than the lecher who turns miser.

II

THE passionate state of mind is often indicative of a lack of skill, talent or power. Moreover, passionate intensity can serve as a substitute for the confidence born of proficiency and the possession of power. A workingman sure of his skill goes leisurely about his job, and accomplishes much though he works as if at play. On the other hand, the workingman who is without confidence attacks his work as if he were saving the world, and he must do so if he is to get anything done. The same is true of the soldier. A well-trained and well-equipped soldier will fight well even when not stirred by strong feeling. But the untrained soldier will give a good account of himself only when animated by enthusiasm and fervor.

12

WHERE there is the necessary technical skill to move mountains, there is no need for the faith that moves mountains.

13

THE times of drastic change are times of passion. We can never be fit and ready for that which is wholly new. We have to adjust ourselves, and every radical adjustment is a crisis in self-esteem: we undergo a test; we have to prove ourselves. A population subjected to drastic change is thus a population of misfits, and misfits live and breathe in an atmosphere of passion.

14

THE soul intensity induced by an inner inadequacy constitutes a release of energy, and it depends on a person's endowments and on attending circumstances whether the released energy works itself out in discontent, in desire, in sheer action or in creativeness.

The chemistry of dissatisfaction is as the chemistry of some marvelously potent tar. In it are the building stones of explosives, stimulants, poisons, opiates, perfumes and stenches.

15

FOR all we know, the wholly harmonious individual might be without the impulse to push on, and without the compulsion to strive for perfection in any department of life. There is always a chance that the perfect society might be a stagnant society.

16

THE best stimulus for running ahead is to have something we must run from.

17

THERE is perhaps no better way of measuring the natural endowment of a soul than by its ability to transmute dissatisfaction into a creative impulse. The genuine artist is as much a dissatisfied person as the revolutionary, yet how diametrically opposed are the products each distills from his dissatisfaction.

18

WE ARE told that talent creates its own opportunities. But it sometimes seems that intense desire creates not only its own opportunities, but its own talents.

19

BY ADEQUATE canalization and under favorable circumstances, any kind of enthusiasm, however crude in nature and origin, can be diverted into creativeness. The enthusiasm born of an error can be canalized into a passionate search for truth.

20

INTENSE desire can be a habit, a fashion or a tradition. It is then apparently unconnected with self-dissatisfaction. Nevertheless, it still retains the structure of its original derivation, and many of the attitudes that are induced by stirring up discontent may also be induced by stimulating sheer desire. The proclivity for change, the receptivity to faith, and the readiness for self-sacrifice are strong both in those who are at war with things as they are, and those who merely desire "more." The fact is that those with the habit of intense desire are only tenuously attached to their lives and possessions. They are, whether they know it or not, the antithesis of the conservative.

21

THERE is radicalism in all getting, and conservatism in all keeping. Lovemaking is radical, while marriage is conservative. So, too, get-rich-quick capitalism is radical, while a capitalism intent solely on keeping what it already has is conservative. Radicalism itself ceases to be radical when absorbed mainly in preserving its control over a society or an economy.

22

"MORE!" is as effective a revolutionary slogan as was ever invented by doctrinaires of discontent. The American, who cannot learn to want what he has, is a permanent revolutionary. He glories in change, has faith in that which he has not yet, and is ready to give his life for it.

23

THERE is a deprecating attitude toward desire among moralists and idealists. They see it as a rushing into "nonentity, absurdity, valuelessness and childishness." Still, the triviality of desire need not impair its value as a motive of human activity. There is no reason why humanity cannot be served equally by weighty and trivial motives. It is indeed doubtful whether it is well for a nation that its people should be so reasonable and earnest that they refuse to set their hearts on toys. The pressure of desire in a population manifests itself in a sort of vigor. There is restlessness, recklessness, sanguineness and aggressiveness. A nation is "tired" when it ceases to want things fervently. It makes no difference whether this blunting of desire is due to satiety, reasonableness or disillusion. To a tired nation the future seems barren, offering nothing which would surpass that which is or has been. The main effect of a real revolution is perhaps that it sweeps away those who do not know how to wish, and brings to the front men with insatiable appetites for action, power and all that the world has to offer.

24

IT IS the awareness of unfulfilled desires which gives a nation the feeling that it has a mission and a destiny.

25

THE propensity to action is symptomatic of an inner unbalance. To be balanced is to be more or less at rest. Action is at bottom a swinging and flailing of the arms to regain one's balance and keep afloat. And if it be true, as Napoleon wrote to Carnot, that "the art of government is not to let men grow stale," then it is an art of unbalancing. The crucial difference between a totalitarian regime and a free social order is perhaps in the methods of unbalancing by which their people are kept active and striving.

26

MEN will try to assert and prove themselves by whatever means and under every sort of condition. A successful social technique consists perhaps in finding unobjectionable means for individual self-assertion.

It is permissible to wonder what other means for the demonstration of individual worth are likely to develop in a nonacquisitive society. Vying in creativity is not a likely substitute for vying in acquisition—not only because creativity is accessible only to the few, but because creative work is without automatic recognition. The nonacquisitive society is likely to develop into a combination of army and school. People will prove themselves by winning citations, degrees, medals and rank. Whatever else we cure by eliminating greed we do not cure life of its triviality.

27

THE independent individual constitutes a chronically unbalanced entity. The confidence and self-esteem which alone can keep him on an even keel are extremely perishable, and must be generated anew each day. An achievement today is but a challenge for tomorrow. When standing at a stay however high he is a prey to nagging fears.

The soul of the autonomous individual has the aspect of a volcanic landscape. There is a seismic line running through it—the line of separation from the self. All our enthusiasms, passionate pursuits, dreams, aspirations and outstanding achievements have their origin along this line of cleavage. The strivings of such a soul are either to heal over the cleavage by a reconciliation with the self through achievement, or camouflage it by self-forgetting, or eliminate it by self-rejection.

28

THERE is a large measure of totalitarianism even in the freest of free societies. But in a free society totalitarianism is not imposed from without but is implanted within the individual. There is a totalitarian regime inside every one of us. We are ruled by a ruthless politburo which sets our norms and drives us from one five-year plan to another. The autonomous individual who has to justify his existence by his own efforts is in eternal bondage to himself.

29

A FATEFUL process is set in motion when the individual is released "to the freedom of his own impotence" and left to justify his existence by his own efforts. The autonomous individual, striving to realize himself and prove his worth, has created all that is great in literature, art, music, science and technology. The autonomous individual, also, when he can neither realize himself nor justify his existence by his own efforts, is a breeding call of frustation, and the seed of the convulsions which shake our world to its foundations. The individual on his own is stable only so long as he is possessed of self-esteem. The maintenance of self-esteem is a continuous task which taxes all of the individual's powers and inner resources. We have to prove our worth and justify our existence anew each day. When, for whatever reason, self-esteem is unattainable, the autonomous individual becomes a highly explosive entity. He turns away from an unpromising self and plunges into the pursuit of pride—the explosive substitute for self-esteem. All social disturbances and upheavals have their roots in crises of individual self-esteem, and the great endeavor in which the masses most readily unite is basically a search for pride.

30

WE ACQUIRE a sense of worth either by realizing our talents, or by keeping busy, or by identifying ourselves with something apart from us—be it a cause, a leader, a group, possessions and the like. Of the three, the path of self-realization is the most difficult. It is taken only when other avenues to a sense of worth are more or less blocked. Men of talent have to be encouraged and goaded to engage in creative work. Their groans and laments echo through the ages.

Action is a highroad to self-confidence and esteem. Where it is open, all energies flow toward it. It comes readily to most people, and its rewards are tangible. The cultivation of the spirit is elusive and difficult, and the tendency toward it is rarely spontaneous. Where the opportunities for action are many, cultural creativeness is likely to be neglected. The cultural flowering of New England came to an almost abrupt end with the opening of the West. The relative cultural sterility of the Romans might perhaps be explained by their empire rather than by an innate lack of genius. The best talents were attracted by the rewards of administrative posts just as the best talents in America are attracted by the rewards of a business career.

31

MAN'S longings are the raw material of his creativeness, his dreams, his excesses, his self-sacrifice, his urge to build and to destroy. A man's soul is pierced as it were with holes, and as his longings flow through each they are transmuted into something specific. The flow through one outlet affects the flow through all the others. Creativeness is a leak, so are dissipation, self-sacrifice, acquisition, the fever of building and the frenzy of destruction; the love of women, of God and of humanity.

32

A SOCIAL order is stable so long as it can give scope to talent and youth. Youth itself is a talent—a perishable talent.

33

THE conditions optimal for cultural creativeness seem to be a marked degree of individual autonomy; a modicum of economic well-being; absence of mass fervor whether religious, patriotic, revolutionary, business or war; a paucity of opportunities for action; a milieu which recognizes and awards merit; and a degree of communal discipline.

The last point needs elucidation.

When people are free to do as they please, they usually imitate each other. Originality is deliberate and forced, and partakes of the nature of a protest. A society which gives unlimited freedom to the individual, more often than not attains a disconcerting sameness. On the other hand, where communal discipline is strict but not ruthless—"an annoyance which irritates, but not a heavy yoke which crushes"—originality is likely to thrive. It is true that when imitation runs its course in a wholly free society it results in a uniformity which is not unlike a mild tyranny. Thus the fully standardized free society has perhaps enough compulsion to challenge originality.

34

WHEN a nation is subject to foreign domination its creativeness is as a rule meager. This is not due to a crippling of the "national genius" but to the fact that resentment against foreign rule so unites a nation that the potentially creative individual cannot attain the distinctness requisite for the full unfolding of his powers. His inner life is tinged and shaped by the feelings and preoccupations of the mass. Like a member of a primitive tribe, he exists not as an individual but as a member of a compact group.

Things are different in the case of resentment against domestic oppression. Provided the oppression is not of the thorough totalitarian brand, the individual may manifest his protest by asserting his distinctness and originality.

35

PRIDE is a sense of worth derived from something that is not organically part of us, while self-esteem derives from the potentialities and achievements of the self. We are proud when we identify ourselves with an imaginary self, a leader, a holy cause, a collective body or possessions. There is fear and intolerance in pride; it is sensitive and uncompromising. The less promise and potency in the self, the more imperative is the need for pride. The core of pride is self-rejection.

It is true that when pride releases energies and serves as a spur to achievement, it can lead to a reconciliation with the self and the attainment of genuine self-esteem.

36

GIVE people pride and they'll live on bread and water, bless their exploiters, and even die for them. Self-surrender is a transaction of barter: we surrender our sense of human dignity, our judgment, our moral and esthetic sense for pride. If there is pride in being free we are ready to die for liberty. If there is pride to be derived from an identification with a leader, we grovel in the dust before a Napoleon, Hitler or Stalin and are ready to die for him. If there is distinction in suffering, we search for martyrdom as for hidden treasure.

37

MONOTHEISM—the adherence to a one and only God, truth, cause, leader, nation and so on—is usually the end result of a search for pride. It was the craving to be a one and only people which impelled the ancient Hebrews to invent a one and only God whose one and only people they were to be.

Whenever we proclaim the uniqueness of a religion, a truth, a leader, a nation, a race, a party or a holy cause, we are also proclaiming our own uniqueness.

38

THE patriotic fervor of a population is not always in direct proportion to its well-being and the fair dealing of its government. Nationalist pride, like other variants of pride, can be a substitute for self-respect. Hence the paradox that when government policies or historical accidents make the attainment and maintenance of individual self-respect difficult, the nationalist spirit of the people becomes more ardent and extreme. The unattainability of individual self-respect is not the least factor behind the chauvinism of the populace in Fascist and Communist regimes.

39

BOTH Faith and Terror are instruments for the elimination of individual self-respect. Terror crushes the autonomy of self-respect, while Faith obtains its more or less voluntary surrender. In both cases the result of the elimination of individual autonomy is —automatism. Both Faith and Terror reduce the human entity to a formula that can be manipulated at will.

40

MAN is indeed a fantastic creature; and nothing about him is so fantastic as the alchemy of his crushed soul which transmutes shame and weakness into pride and faith.

41

IT HAS been often said that power corrupts. But it is perhaps equally important to realize that weakness, too, corrupts. Power corrupts the few, while weakness corrupts the many. Hatred, malice, rudeness, intolerance, and suspicion are the fruits of weakness. The resentment of the weak does not spring from any injustice done to them but from the sense of their inadequacy and impotence. They hate not wickedness but weakness. When it is in their power to do so, the weak destroy weakness wherever they see it. Woe to the weak when they are preyed upon by the weak. The self-hatred of the weak is likewise an instance of their hatred of weakness.

42

NOTE also how perverse is the attitude of the weak toward their benefactors. They feel generosity as oppression; they want to retaliate. They say to their benefactors: "May the day come when you shall be weak and we will send bundles to America."

You do not win the weak by sharing your wealth with them; it will but infect them with greed and resentment. You can win the weak only by sharing your pride, hope or hatred with them.

43

THE mere possession of power does not inevitably lead to aggression. It is when power is wedded to chronic fear that it becomes formidable. Some inner unbalance is apparently needed to keep people on the go, and it needs the unbalancing of fear to activate power.

Another way of putting it would be that only when power utilizes the propensities and talents of the weak does it become ruthless and vicious.

44

GREAT evils befall the world when the powerful begin to copy the weak. The desperate devices which enable the weak to survive are unequaled instruments of oppression and extermination in the hands of the strong.

45

UNLIKE the pattern which seems to prevail in the rest of life, in the human species the weak not only survive but often triumph over the strong. The self-hatred inherent in the weak unlocks energies far more formidable than those mobilized by an ordinary struggle for existence. The shifts and devices the weak employ to escape an untenable reality are often preposterous, yet they somehow turn out to be generators of power. One thinks of the magic of words which turns thin air into absolute truths, and the alchemy of conviction which transmutes self-contempt into pride, lack of confidence into faith, and a sense of guilt into self-righteousness. Finally, self-hatred endows the weak with an exceptional facility for united action. Flight from the self almost invariably turns into a rush for a compact group. And certainly, this readiness to unite with others is a source of unequaled strength. Thus the soul intensity generated in the weak endows them as it were with a special fitness. There is sober realism in St. Paul's stilted words that: "God hath chosen the weak things of the world to confound the things that are mighty."

46

THAT self-hatred should generate in us an eagerness to unite with others seems to suggest that it is primarily against ourselves that we league ourselves with others.

47

BY RENOUNCING the self we are getting out from underneath the only burden that is real. For however much we identify ourselves with a holy cause, our fears on its behalf can never be as real and poignant as our fear and trembling in behalf of a perishable self. The short-lived self, teetering on the edge of irrevocable extinction, is the only thing that can ever really matter. Thus the renunciation of the self is felt as a liberation and salvation.

48

RELIGION is not a matter of God, church, holy cause, etc. These are but accessories. The source of religious preoccupation is in the self, or rather the rejection of the self. Dedication is the obverse side of self-rejection. Man alone is a religious animal because, as Montaigne points out, "it is a malady confined to man, and not seen in any other creature, to hate and despise ourselves."

49

IT IS a talent of the weak to persuade themselves that they suffer for something when they suffer from something; that they are showing the way when they are running away; that they see the light when they feel the heat; that they are chosen when they are shunned.

50

THE formidableness and uniqueness of the human species stem from the survival of its weak. Were it not for the habit of caring for the sick, the crippled and the weak in general humanity could not have perhaps attained to culture and civilization. The invalided warrior who had to stay behind while the manhood of the tribe went out to war was probably the first storyteller, teacher and artisan (fashioning weapons and toys). The earliest development of religion, poetry and wit owed much to the survival of the unfit. One thinks of the unhinged medicine man, the epileptic prophet, the blind bard, the witty hunchback and dwarf. Finally, the sick must have had a hand in the development of the arts of healing and cooking.

51

T H E exceptional adaptability of the human species is chiefly a peculiarity of its weak. The difficult and risky task of meeting and mastering the new—whether it be the settlement of new lands or the initiation of new ways of life—is not undertaken by the vanguard of a society but by its rear. It is the misfits, failures, fugitives, outcasts and their like who are among the first to grapple with the new. Only when, after a clumsy and wasteful struggle, they have somehow bound and tamed the unknown do their betters move in and take charge. The plunge into the new is often an escape from a familiar pattern that is untenable and unpleasant. It is the weak who strain their ears for a new word, clutch at every promise and rally around a savior and a redeemer.

The role the unfit play in human affairs should make us pause whenever we are prompted to see man as a mere animal and not a being of an order apart.

52

WE ALMOST always prove something when we act heroically. We prove to ourselves and others that we are not what we and they thought we were. Our real self is petty, greedy, cowardly, dishonest and stewing in malice. And now in defying death and spitting in its eye we grasp at the chance of a grand refutation.

53

TO ACT or think extremely one needs a sense of the dramatic. Excesses are essentially gestures. It is easy to be extremely cruel, magnanimous, humble or self-sacrificing when we see ourselves actors in a performance.

54

IT SOMETIMES seems that our most persistent and passionate effort is to convince the world that we are not what we really are.

God alone is satisfied with what He is and can proclaim: "I am what I am." Unlike God, man strives with all his might to be what he is not. He incessantly proclaims: "I am what I am not."

55

THE moment we are seized with a passion to be different from what we are, we are in a religious mood. Remorse, a vivid awareness of our weakness and worthlessness, the craving for pride and fame—they all involve a reaching out for a new identity, and they all have a religious nexus.

56

MAKE-BELIEVE partakes of the nature of a magic ritual. We not only pretend to be what we are not, but by staging our pretense we strive to conjure and bring into existence a new genuineness. The strange thing is that often this conjuring act succeeds, and we become what we pretend to be.

57

OUR most poignant frustrations can be traced back to something in us that puts an insurmountable limit to our capacity for make-believe. If our skin be black, our back hunched, our creative capacity manifestly meager we feel as if we were chained and imprisoned.

58

FAR more crucial than what we know or do not know is what we do not want to know. One often obtains a clue to a person's nature by discovering the reasons for his or her imperviousness to certain impressions.

59

IT IS as though our inner self is always in a state of war. No totalitarian censor can approach the implacability of the censor who controls the line of communication between the outer world and our consciousness. Nothing is allowed to reach us which might weaken our confidence and lower our morale. To most of us nothing is so invisible as an unpleasant truth. Though it is held before our eyes, pushed under our noses, rammed down our throats—we know it not.

60

THE fact seems to be that we are least open to precise knowledge concerning the things we are most vehement about. The rabid radical remains in the dark concerning the nature of radicalism, and the religious concerning the nature of religion.

Vehemence is the expression of a blind effort to support and uphold something that can never stand on its own—something rootless, incoherent and incomplete. Whether it is our own meaningless self we are upholding or some doctrine devoid of evidence, we can do it only in a frenzy of faith.

61

THE weakness of a soul is proportionate to the number of truths that must be kept from it.

62

IF WHAT we profess is not an organic part of our understanding, we are likely to profess it with vehemence and intolerance. Intolerance is the "Do Not Touch" sign on something that cannot bear touching. We do not mind having our hair ruffled, but we will not tolerate any familiarity with the toupee which covers our baldness.

63

THE uncompromising attitude is more indicative of an inner uncertainty than of deep conviction. The implacable stand is directed more against the doubt within than the assailant without.

64

WHAT is farthest removed from our flesh-and-blood selves?

Words.

To attach people to words is to detach them most effectively from life and possessions, and thus ready them for reckless acts of self-sacrifice. Men will fight and die for a word more readily than for anything else. The metaphysical double-talk which has fascinated the Germans since the days of Hegel was undoubtedly a factor in the rise of that German recklessness which has shaken our world to its foundations. At present, Communist double-talk is moving millions in Europe and Asia to acts of daring and self-sacrifice.

They are dangerous times when words are everything.

65

IT IS by their translation into mere words and almost meaningless symbols that ideas move people and stir them to action. This deintellectualization of ideas is the work of the pseudo-intellectuals. The self-styled intellectual who is impotent with pen and ink hungers to write history with sword and blood.

66

THERE are people who need the sanction —or rather the incantation—of an idea in order to be able to act. They want to command, manage and conquer; but they must feel that in satisfying these passions and hungers they do not cater to the despised self but are engaged in the solemn ritual of making the word become flesh. Usually, such people are without the capacity to originate ideas. Their special talent lies rather in the deintellectualization of ideas—the turning of ideas into slogans and battle cries which beget action.

67

QUITE often in history action has been the echo of words. An era of talk was followed by an era of events.

The new barbarism of the twentieth century is the echo of words bandied about by brilliant speakers and writers in the second half of the nineteenth.

68

A DOCTRINE insulates the devout not only against the realities around them but also against their own selves. The fanatical believer is not conscious of his envy, malice, pettiness and dishonesty. There is a wall of words between his consciousness and his real self.

69

WE OFTEN use strong language not to express a powerful emotion or conviction but to evoke it in us. It is not only other people's words that can rouse feeling in us; we can talk ourselves into a rage or an enthusiasm.

70

WE LIE loudest when we lie to ourselves.

71

THERE are many who have grave scruples about deceiving others but think it as nothing to deceive themselves. Still, it is doubtful whether the self-deceivers can ever really tell the truth.

72

TO THE self-despisers reality is soiled and threadbare. They cannot base their opinions on the evidence of their senses. They are reluctant to distill their judgment of a country, a government or of humanity in general from the raw material of their daily experience.

73

THE war on the present is usually a war on facts. Facts are the toys of men who live and die at leisure. They who are engrossed in the rapid realization of an extravagant hope tend to view facts as something base and unclean. Facts are counterrevolutionary.

74

WE CANNOT dream passionately of the future without making a counterfeit of the present. The craving for things that are not induces us to see the world as it is not.

75

THE remarkable thing is that a preoccupation with the future not only prevents us from seeing the present as it is but often prompts us to rearrange the past. To enter the realm of the future is like entering a foreign country: one must have a passport, and one must be able to provide a detailed record of one's past. Thus a nation's preoccupation with history is not unfrequently an effort to obtain a passport for the future. Often it is a forged passport.

76

IT SEEMS that when we concentrate for a time on something that is new and difficult we acquire a sense of foreignness which we carry over as we shift to familiar fields. Thus it happens that those who set their minds on tackling the wholly new often end up by seeing the familiar as if it were new and difficult, and expend their energies in directing and regulating affairs which usually function automatically.

77

A LIVING faith is basically faith in the future. Hence he who would inspire faith must give the impression that he can peer into the future, and that everything that is happening under his guidance —even when it turns out disastrously—had been foreseen and foretold.

78

THE only way to predict the future is to have power to shape the future. Those in possession of absolute power can not only prophesy and make their prophecies come true, but they can also lie and make their lies come true.

79

THOSE who are in love with the present can be cruel and corrupt but not genuinely vicious. They cannot be methodically and consistently ruthless.

80

RUDENESS seems somehow linked with a rejection of the present. When we reject the present we also reject ourselves—we are, so to speak, rude toward ourselves; and we usually do unto others what we have already done to ourselves.

81

TO THE child, the savage and the Wall Street operator everything seems possible—hence their credulity. The same is true of people who live in times of great uncertainty. Both fear and hope promote credulity. And it is perhaps true that those who want to create a state of mind receptive to fantastic and manifestly absurd tenets should preach hope and also create a feeling of insecurity.

82

EVERYTHING seems possible when we are absolutely helpless or absolutely powerful—and both states stimulate our credulity.

83

THE charlatan is not usually a cynical individual who preys on the credulous. It is the credulous themselves who manifest a propensity for charlatanism. When we believe ourselves in possession of the only truth, we are likely to be indifferent to common everyday truths.

Self-deception, credulity and charlatanism are somehow linked together.

84

MODERN man is weighed down more by the burden of responsibility than by the burden of sin. We think him more a savior who shoulders our responsibilites than him who shoulders our sins. If instead of making decisions we have but to obey and do our duty, we feel it as a sort of salvation.

85

THERE is a powerful craving in most of us to see ourselves as instruments in the hands of others and thus free ourselves from the responsibility for acts which are prompted by our own questionable inclinations and impulses. Both the strong and the weak grasp at this alibi. The latter hide their malevolence under the virtue of obedience: they acted dishonorably because they had to obey orders. The strong, too, claim absolution by proclaiming themselves the chosen instrument of a higher power—God, history, fate, nation or humanity.

86

THE awareness that the misfortunes which befall us are some sort of retribution for past transgressions often evokes in us a sense of relief. We are relieved of immediate responsibility for whatever it is that is happening to us. For if our difficulties can be ascribed to something that has happened in the past, they cannot serve as evidence of our present inadequacy and cannot blemish our self-confidence and self-esteem.

87

FEAR comes from uncertainty. When we are absolutely certain, whether of our worth or worthlessness, we are almost impervious to fear. Thus a feeling of utter unworthiness can be a source of courage.

88

ABSOLUTE power is partial to simplicity. It wants simple problems, simple solutions, simple definitions. It sees in complication a product of weakness—the torturous path compromise must follow. There is thus a certain similarity between the pattern of extremism and that of absolute power.

89

WE ASSOCIATE brittleness and vulnerability with those we love, while we endow those we hate with strength and indestructibility. It is perhaps true that the first conception of an almighty God had its origin in the visualization of an implacable enemy rather than a friendly protector. Men loved God the way the Russians loved Stalin. Only by convincing ourselves that we really and truly love an all-powerful and all-seeing enemy can we be sure of never betraying ourselves by a word or gesture. "How are you going to love," said Tertullian, "unless you are afraid not to love!"

90

OUR sense of power is more vivid when we break a man's spirit than when we win his heart. For we can win a man's heart one day and lose it the next. But when we break a proud spirit we achieve something that is final and absolute.

91

WHEN the weak want to give an impression of strength they hint meaningfully at their capacity for evil. It is by its promise of a sense of power that evil often attracts the weak.

92

THE paradox is that much that is achieved by faith can also be achieved by utmost frivolity. If faith rejects the present, frivolity makes light of it and disregards it. Both the devout and the utterly frivolous are capable of self-sacrifice. Both generate a fortitude which sustains one in difficulties; both are capable of extremes.

93

THE fact of death and nothingness at the end is a certitude unsurpassed by any absolute truth ever discovered. Yet knowing this, people can be deadly serious about their prospects, grievances, duties and trespassings. The only explanation which suggests itself is that seriousness is a means of camouflage: we conceal the triviality and nullity of our lives by taking things seriously. No opiate and no pleasure chase can so effectively mask the terrible truth about man's life as does seriousness.

94

CONSIDERING how lighthearted we feel when we do not take ourselves seriously, it is surprising how difficult the attainment of this sensible and practical attitude seems to be. It is apparently much easier to be serious than frivolous.

95

HISTORY is made by men who have the restlessness, impressionability, credulity, capacity for make-believe, ruthlessness and self-righteousness of children. It is made by men who set their hearts on toys. All leaders strive to turn their followers into children.

96

MAN'S being is neither profound nor sublime. To search for something deep underneath the surface in order to explain human phenomena is to discard the nutritious outer layer for a nonexistent core. Like a bulb man is all skin and no kernel.

97

MAN is eminently a storyteller. His search for a purpose, a cause, an ideal, a mission and the like is largely a search for a plot and a pattern in the development of his life story—a story that is basically without meaning or pattern.

The turning of our lives into a story is also a means of rousing the interest of others in us and associating them with us.

98

ACTION can give us the feeling of being useful, but only words can give us a sense of weight and purpose.

99

AN EASYGOING person is probably more accessible to a realization of eternity—the endless flow of life and death—than one who takes his prospects and duties overseriously. It is the overserious who are truly frivolous.

100

THE remarkable thing is that we really love our neighbor as ourselves: we do unto others as we do unto ourselves. We hate others when we hate ourselves. We are tolerant toward others when we tolerate ourselves. We forgive others when we forgive ourselves. We are prone to sacrifice others when we are ready to sacrifice ourselves.

It is not love of self but hatred of self which is at the root of the troubles that afflict our world.

101

I T I S an evil thing to expect too much either from ourselves or from others. Disappointment in ourselves does not moderate our expectations from others; on the contrary, it raises them. It is as if we wished to be disappointed with our fellow men.

One does not really love mankind when one expects too much from them.

102

THE craving to change the world is perhaps a reflection of the craving to change ourselves. The untenability of a situation does not by itself always give rise to a desire for change. Our quarrel with the world is an echo of the endless quarrel proceeding within us. The revolutionary agitator must first start a war in every soul before he can find recruits for his war with the world.

103

THOUGH the reformer is seen as a champion of change, he actually looks down on anything that can be changed. Only that which is corrupt and inferior must be subjected to the treatment of change. The reformer prides himself on the possession of an eternal unchangeable truth. It is his hostility toward things as they are which goads him to change them; he is as it were inflicting on them an indignity. Hence his passion for change is not infrequently a destructive passion.

104

THE sick in soul insist that it is humanity that is sick, and they are the surgeons to operate on it. They want to turn the world into a sickroom. And once they get humanity strapped to the operating table, they operate on it with an ax.

105

WERE one to invent a pill which if taken before going to bed would transform men overnight into patterns of perfection, the reformer would be the unhappiest man on earth. The reformer wants to play a role; he wants to make history.

106

THERE is always a chance that he who sets himself up as his brother's keeper will end up by being his jailkeeper.

107

THERE is perhaps in all misfits a powerful secret craving to turn the whole of humanity into misfits. Hence partly their passionate advocacy of a drastically new social order. For we are all misfits when we have to adjust ourselves to the wholly new.

108

OUR power over the world is far greater than we dream. We fashion everything we touch in our own image.

109

DEEP within us there is a conviction that every mother's son is better than we. Our self-righteousness is an echo of this conviction. Do we not expect others to be ashamed of thoughts and deeds which we ourselves think and do without embarrassment?

110

WHEN we are conscious of our worthlessness, we naturally expect others to be finer and better than we are. If then we discover any similarity between them and us, we see it as irrefutable evidence of their worthlessness and inferiority. It is thus that with some people familiarity breeds contempt.

111

WHAT greater reassurance can the weak have than that they are like anyone else?

112

BY DISCOVERING our own blemishes in others we as it were assert our kinship with others. Malice is thus a social faculty.

113

THE pleasure we derive from doing favors is partly in the feeling it gives us that we are not altogether worthless. It is a pleasant surprise to ourselves.

114

TO BE truly selfish one needs a degree of self-esteem. The self-despisers are less intent on their own increase than on the diminution of others. Where self-esteem is unattainable, envy takes the place of greed.

115

THE real "haves" are they who can acquire freedom, self-confidence and even riches without depriving others of them. They acquire all of these by developing and applying their potentialities. On the other hand, the real "have nots" are they who cannot have aught except by depriving others of it. They can feel free only by diminishing the freedom of others, self-confident by spreading fear and dependence among others, and rich by making others poor.

116

RESENTMENT springs more from a sense of weakness than from a sense of injustice. We resent a wholly false accusation less than one which is partly justified. The blameless are perhaps incapable of resentment.

117

THE attempt to justify an evil deed has perhaps more pernicious consequences than the evil deed itself. The justification of a past crime is the planting and cultivation of future crimes. Indeed, the repetition of a crime is sometimes part of a device of justification: we do it again and again to convince ourselves and others that it is a common thing and not an enormity.

118

SOMETIMES when we accuse others we are actually excusing ourselves. The more we need to justify ourselves, the greater will be our self-righteousness.

119

MAN feels truly at ease only when he pities. His love and admiration for his equals and betters is beset with misgiving. Sometimes, indeed, we convince ourselves of the innate weakness of others for no better reason but that we may love them unreservedly.

120

WE DERIVE a certain satisfaction from being sinned against. It is not only that a grievance adds content to our lives, but also that it makes less monstrous the flame of malice which like a vigil light flickers in the dimness of our souls.

121

HOWEVER unjust and unreasonable the attitude we assume toward others, we seem to set in motion an automatic process which works blindly to corroborate and justify that attitude. It is an awesome thing that when we expose people, however undeservedly, to hatred, they tend to become hateful. Our prejudices, suspicions and lies have this power to compel souls into a conforming pattern. It is as if the world, of its own accord, furnishes reasons for our unreasonable attitudes.

122

THERE is in human affairs a reciprocity and an equilibrium between cause and effect. The cause can be as much affected by the effect, as the effect is produced by the cause. Indeed, it is often possible to produce the cause by staging the effect.

Whatever of good or evil we start in life will tend to justify and perpetuate itself.

123

IT IS futile to judge a kind deed by its motives. Kindness can become its own motive. We are made kind by being kind.

124

IT WOULD be difficult to exaggerate the degree to which we are influenced by those we influence.

125

IT SEEMS that the more unjustified a persecution, the more vehement and lasting is it likely to be. An unjust persecution ends only when the innocent victim is wiped off the face of the earth. An intense feeling of guilt is almost indistinguishable from blind faith; it fosters the same ruthlessness and persistence. And just as the intensity and persistence of a faith cannot be accepted as proof of its truth, so the intensity and persistence of a persecution cannot be cited as evidence of its justness.

126

TO FIND the cause of our ills in something outside ourselves, something specific that can be spotted and eliminated, is a diagnosis that cannot fail to appeal. To say that the cause of our troubles is not in us but in the Jews, and pass immediately to the extermination of the Jews, is a prescription likely to find a wide acceptance.

127

THERE is something of the irresistibility of a chemical reaction—something that proceeds independently of our consciousness and will—in the penetration of a generally held opinion and its tinging of our inner life. That which corrodes the souls of the persecuted is the monstrous inner agreement with the prevailing prejudice against them.

128

OUR credulity is greatest concerning the things we know least about. And since we know least about ourselves, we are ready to believe all that is said about us. Hence the mysterious power of both flattery and calumny.

129

IT IS thus with most of us: we are what other people say we are. We know ourselves chiefly by hearsay.

130

THE people we meet are the playwrights and stage managers of our lives: they cast us in a role, and we play it whether we will or not. It is not so much the example of others we imitate as the reflection of ourselves in their eyes and the echo of ourselves in their words.

131

THE readiness to praise others indicates a desire for excellence and perhaps an ability to realize it.

132

A SOUL that is reluctant to share does not as a rule have much of its own. Miserliness is here a symptom of meagerness.

133

THOSE who are ready to praise others usually take praise from others with a grain of salt. On the other hand, those who praise others reluctantly accept praise from others at its face value. Thus the less magnanimous a soul, the more readily does it succumb to flattery.

134

WHEN we are not governed too much by what other people think of us, we are likely to be tolerant toward the behavior and the opinions of others. So, too, when we do not crave to seem important we are not awed by the importance of others. Both our fear and intolerance are the result of our dependence.

135

OUR impulse to persuade others is strongest when we have to persuade ourselves. The never wholly successful task of persuading ourselves of our worth manifests itself in a ceaseless effort to persuade others of it.

136

WE HAVE more faith in what we imitate than in what we originate. We cannot derive a sense of absolute certitude from anything which has its roots in us. The most poignant sense of insecurity comes from standing alone; we are not alone when we imitate.

137

A VALID index by which to evaluate the influence other people have on us is by how much they increase or dimininsh our benevolence toward our fellow men.

138

ONE of the best reasons for guarding ourselves against doing harm to anyone is to preserve our capacity for compassion. For we cannot pity those we have wronged.

139

COMPASSION is probably the only antitoxin of the soul. Where there is compassion even the most poisonous impulses are relatively harmless. One would rather see the world run by men who set their hearts on toys but are accessible to pity, than by men animated by lofty ideals whose dedication makes them ruthless. In the chemistry of man's soul, almost all noble attributes—courage, honor, hope, faith, duty, loyalty, etc.—can be transmuted into ruthlessness. Compassion alone stands apart from the continuous traffic between good and evil proceeding within us.

140

IT IS compassion rather than the principle of justice which can guard us against being unjust to our fellow men.

-

141

GOOD judgment in our dealings with others consists not in seeing through deceptions and evil intentions but in being able to waken the decency dormant in every person.

142

THE taint hidden in selflessness is that self-lessness is the only moral justification of ruthlessness.

143

ORIGINAL sin? It is probably the malice that is ever flickering within us. Seen thus, it is a grievous error for those who manage human affairs not to take original sin into account.

144

MEN of strong passions are usually without compassion. The feeling for others is "a still small voice" that makes itself heard only in the quiet of an inner equilibrium. The passion for humanity even is not infrequently lacking in humanity.

145

TO BE fruitful, an enthusiasm should be but as a condiment. Pride in our country and race, dedication to justice, freedom, mankind, etc., must never be the main content of our lives, but an accompaniment and an accessory.

146

THOSE who would sacrifice a generation to realize an ideal are the enemies of mankind.

147

THE only index by which to judge a government or a way of life is by the quality of the people it acts upon. No matter how noble the objectives of a government, if it blurs decency and kindness, cheapens human life, and breeds ill will and suspicion—it is an evil government.

148

IT IS doubtful whether we can reform human beings by eliminating their undesirable traits. In most cases elimination comes to nothing more than substitution: we substitute a close relative for the bad trait we have eliminated, and the dynasty continues. Envy takes the place of greed, self-righteousness that of selfishness, intellectual dishonesty that of plain dishonesty. And there is always a chance that the new bad trait will be more vigorous than the one it supplants.

149

THERE is always a danger that the suppression of a specific clearly defined evil will result in its replacement by an evil that is widely diffused—one that infects the whole fabric of life. Thus the suppression of religious fanaticism usually gives rise to a secular fanaticism that invades every department of life. The banning of conventional warmaking may result in an endless undeclared war. The elimination of the conventional employer gives rise to a general monstrosity that bosses not only our working hours but invades our homes and dictates our thoughts and dreams.

150

IN THIS godless age, as much as in any preceding religious age, man is still preoccupied with the saving of his soul. The discrediting of established religions by enlightenment did not result in a weakening of the religious impulse. A traditional religion canalizes and routinizes the quest for salvation. When such a religion is discredited, the individual must do his own soul-saving, and he is at it twenty-four hours a day. There is an eruption of fanaticism in all departments of life—in business, politics, literature, art, science and even in lovemaking and sport. The elimination of the sacerdotal outlet results thus in a general infection and inflammation of the social body.

151

TO BECOME different from what we are, we must have some awareness of what we are. Whether this being different results in dissimulation or a real change of heart—it cannot be realized without self-awareness.

Yet it is remarkable that the very people who are most self-dissatisfied and crave most for a new identity have the least self-awareness. They have turned away from an unwanted self and hence never had a good look at it. The result is that the most dissatisfied can neither dissimulate nor attain a real change of heart. They are transparent, and their unwanted qualities persist through all attempts at self-dramatization and self-transformation.

152

LACK of sensitivity is perhaps basically an unawareness of ourselves.

153

THE inability to see into ourselves often manifests itself in a certain coarseness and clumsiness. One can be brazen, rude and even dishonest without being aware of it.

154

THOSE who remain in the dark about their own motives are as it were strangers to themselves. Hence perhaps their exceptional power of self-delusion —their ability to talk themselves into anything. Their own impassioned words affect their souls as the words of an outside propagandist.

155

THERE are people who seem continually engaged in an effort of self-proselytizing. To whomever they may talk or write it is to themselves they are talking or writing. They are continually engaged in talking or writing themselves into a conviction, an enthusiasm or an illusion.

156

THE chief taint of self-righteousness is not its injustice but its insensitivity. The indulgence of self-forgiving is far less vicious than the blindness of self-righteousness which is not aware of aught in the self that needs forgiving.

157

LACK of self-awareness renders us transparent. A soul that knows itself is opaque; like Adam after he ate from the tree of knowledge it uses words as fig leaves to cover its nakedness and shame.

158

WE CAN see through others only when we see through ourselves.

159

NO ONE is truly literate who cannot read his own heart.

160

THE most sensitive among us cannot be as observant of themselves as the least sensitive are observant of others.

161

IT WILL perhaps never be possible to speak about our inner life in precise scientific terms. Can one laugh at oneself or pity oneself in scientific terminology? The choice is between poetry and aphorism. The latter is probably the less vague.

162

IT IS perhaps true that each era demands a particular kind of God. There are eras when people can believe in a God far off in heaven, never to be seen, and eras when they need a tangible God. Our age, it seems, needs a tangible God, be it a Hitler, a Stalin, or a Father Divine.

Is this primitive need for a tangible God somehow connected with lack of faith in the future? The ancient Jews, who were the first to have faith in an invisible God, were possessed of a vivid faith in the future. Alone among the nations of antiquity they expected the future to surpass present and past. Apparently when we hope "for what we see not," we can also believe in what we see not. It is perhaps a symptom of the hopelessness of our times that we need idols to worship.

163

SOME generations have patience and some are without it. This is one of the most crucial differences between eras. There is a time when the word "eventually" has the soothing effect of a promise, and a time when the word evokes in us bitterness and scorn.

164

WE ARE not worried about our footing when we are about to jump. It is when we have nowhere to jump that we begin to worry about the soundness of our position. They who go places give no thought to security.

165

WHEN we have no faith in the future we incline to arrange our lives so that we can predict the future. We either make of our existence a rigid routine or pile up all manner of defenses to make it secure. The craving for security stems from a need for predictability, and its intensity is in inverse proportion to our faith in the future.

166

TO HAVE a grievance is to have a purpose in life. A grievance can almost serve as a substitute for hope; and it not infrequently happens that those who hunger for hope give their allegiance to him who offers them a grievance.

167

IT IS remarkable by how much a pinch of malice enhances the penetrating power of an idea or an opinion. Our ears, it seems, are wonderfully attuned to sneers and evil reports about our fellow men.

168

OF ALL the ways of filling one's life and of creating the illusion of purpose and worth, none seems so effective as the voluntary subjugation to a set of duties. The satisfaction derived from the daily performance of duties is so unalloyed that the inclination is strong to pile duty upon duty and revel in their performance.

169

THERE is a grandeur in the uniformity of the mass. When a fashion, a dance, a song, a slogan or a joke sweeps like wildfire from one end of the continent to the other, and a hundred million people roar with laughter, sway their bodies in unison, hum one song or break forth in anger and denunciation, there is the overpowering feeling that in this country we have come nearer the brotherhood of man than ever before.

170

IN AMERICA not only are class lines indistinct but there is something at work which equalizes people irrespective of their education, possessions, occupations and their mental and physical attributes. The differences are relatively slight between the educated and the uneducated, the rich and the poor, soldiers and civilians, old and young, men and women, business leaders and labor leaders, the sane and the insane, and (considering the quantities of patent medicines consumed by all) the healthy and the sick.

171

YOU cannot gauge the intelligence of an American by talking with him; you must work with him. The American polishes and refines his way of doing things—even the most commonplace—the way the French of the seventeenth century polished their maxims and aphorisms.

172

THE superficiality of the American is the result of his hustling. It needs leisure to think things out; it needs leisure to mature. People in a hurry cannot think, cannot grow, nor can they decay. They are preserved in a state of perpetual puerility.

173

A PUSH-BUTTON civilization has no feeling for change by growth—the change that proceeds quietly, and by degrees scarcely to be perceived. The remarkable thing is that the theologian, too, has no feeling for development by growth. His conception of creation and change is as much a push-button affair as that of the technician and the revolutionary.

174

IT IS the homesick who keep shifting about. The uprooted millions from Europe who landed on our shores were certainly not the cosmopolitan type who transplant well. They remained homesick all their lives and kept moving westward.

The Jews, homesick for the Promised Land, have been on the move for two thousand years.

175

THE nonconformist is a more stable type than the conforming individual. It is the average man of today who shows the most striking differences from people of other ages and other civilizations. The rebel of today is twin brother of rebels in all ages and climes.

176

THE basic test of freedom is perhaps less in what we are free to do than in what we are free not to do. It is the freedom to refrain, withdraw and abstain which makes a totalitarian regime impossible. Those addicted to action do not probably feel unfree in an active totalitarian regime. Hitler won over the generals, technicians and scientists not by preaching to them but by giving them more than they asked for and encouraging them to go the limit.

177

WHEN we are in competition with ourselves, and match our todays against our yesterdays, we derive encouragement from past misfortunes and blemishes. Moreover, the competition with ourselves leaves unimpaired our benevolence toward our fellow men.

178

OUR preoccupation with other people—whether we aid or hinder them, love or hate them—is at bottom a means of getting away from ourselves. It is strange to contemplate that competition with others—the breathless race to get ahead of others—is basically a running away from ourselves.

179

WHEN a situation is so unprecedented that no amount of knowledge or experience is adequate to master it, then the ignorant and inexperienced are more fit to deal with it than the learned and experienced. The unknown and untried give as it were a special fitness to the unfit.

180

THE discovery and elaboration of new forms of expression whether in literature, art or music are often the work of the least talented. The search for a new form of expression is often an attempt to camouflage the fact that one has nothing new to express. However, once the new form is worked out, it is seized upon by the talented, and it is only then that the new manner begins to manifest force, beauty and originality.

It is often the failure who is a pioneer in new lands, new undertakings, and new forms of expression.

181

THERE are many who find a good alibi far more attractive than an achievement. For an achievement does not settle anything permanently. We still have to prove our worth anew each day: we have to prove that we are as good today as we were yesterday. But when we have a valid alibi for not achieving anything we are fixed, so to speak, for life. Moreover, when we have an alibi for not writing a book, painting a picture and so on, we have an alibi for not writing the greatest book and not painting the greatest picture. Small wonder that the effort expended and the punishment endured in obtaining a good alibi often exceed the effort and grief requisite for the attainment of a most marked achievement.

182

WHEN we say that there is a deeper reason for this or that, we usually mean that there is a less worthy reason. We expect the ugly and the base to be hidden from sight. The deep insight and the profound saying touch mostly upon that which is not above reproach.

183

FEAR and guilt are usually closely associated. They who feel guilty are afraid, and they who are afraid somehow feel guilty. To the onlooker, too, the fearful seem guilty.

184

RABID suspicion has nothing in it of skepticism. The suspicious mind believes more than it doubts. It believes in a formidable and ineradicable evil lurking in every person.

185

WE ARE likely to have a regard for the opinion of others only when there is a chance that the opinion might be now and then in our favor.

The Negro who is convinced that public opinion will be against him, no matter how he acts, often behaves like a spoiled society lady who does not give a damn what people think of her.

186

IT IS impossible to think clearly in under-statements. Thought is a process of exaggeration. The refusal to exaggerate is not infrequently an alibi for the disinclination to think or praise.

187

WHEN we are engrossed in a struggle for sheer survival, the self occupies the center of the stage; it is as it were our holy cause. Selflessness is then mean-ingless. The enthusiasm of self-surrender can rise only when we no longer have to strive for physical survival.

188

THE wisdom of others remains dull till it is writ over with our own blood. We are essentially apart from the world; it bursts into our consciousness only when it sinks its teeth and nails into us.

189

AS THE world pokes its fingers into our souls, it now and then touches bedrock: something compact, real, unequivocal. And whether it be genuine disgust, joy, grief, pity, shame or desire—it is accompanied by a vague sense of gratification. We are gratified by the discovery that we are not all sham and show, that there are elements in our inner make-up as organically our own as the color of our eyes and the shape of our nose. For we are never really sure of the genuineness of our convictions, feelings, tastes and desires. We are rarely free of the suspicion that we are "making a show." Hence the discovery of something autochthonous within us gives us a sense of uniqueness.

190

THE mortification born of a shameful act does not usually last long. With most people it passes within forty-eight hours. And yet each mortification as it passes leaves a stain and a blemish on our feeling of well-being. Thus gradually an undercurrent of self-contempt begins coursing within us, and now and then it leaks out in bitterness and hatred toward others. It is in rare moments when we have a particular reason to be satisfied with ourselves that we realize the depression and dejection secreted in us by a guilty conscience.

191

SECRETIVENESS can be a source of pride. It is a paradox that secretiveness plays the same role as boasting: both are engaged in the creation of a disguise. Boasting tries to create an imaginary self, while secretiveness gives us the exhilarating feeling of being princes disguised in meekness. Of the two, secretiveness is the more difficult and effective. For in the self-observant boasting breeds self-contempt. Yet it is as Spinoza said: "Men govern nothing with more difficulty than their tongues, and can moderate their desires more than their words."

192

BY ACCUSING others of a crime we committed or are about to commit, we drain all force from any accusation which may be leveled against us. We attach a quality of hollowness and incredibility to the formula of indictment.

193

IF WHAT we do and feel today is not in harmony with what we want to be tomorrow, the meeting with our hope at the end of the trail is likely to be embarrassing or even hostile. Thus it often happens that a man slays his hope even as he battles for it.

194

THE desire to be different from the people we live with is sometimes the result of our rejection —real or imagined—by them.

We often hate that which we cannot be. We put up defenses against something we crave and cannot have.

195

THERE is in us a dark craving for rot. It is as if decay were an escape from the limits, the oppressive fears and the pains of an individual existence.

196

THE control of our being is not unlike the combination of a safe. One turn of the knob rarely unlocks the safe. Each advance and retreat is a step toward one's goal.

197

CONSERVATISM is sometimes a symptom of sterility. Those who have nothing in them that can grow and develop must cling to what they have in beliefs, ideas and possessions. The sterile radical, too, is basically conservative. He is afraid to let go of the ideas and beliefs he picked up in his youth lest his life be seen as empty and wasted.

198

WE CLAMOR for equality chiefly in matters in which we ourselves cannot hope to attain excellence. To discover what a man truly craves but knows he cannot have we must find the field in which he advocates absolute equality. By this test the Communists are frustrated Capitalists.

199

IF WE want people to behave in a certain manner, we must set the stage and give them a cue. This is true also when it is ourselves we want to induce. There is no telling how deeply a mind may be affected by the deliberate staging of gestures, acts and symbols.

Pretense is often an indispensable step in the attainment of genuineness. It is a form into which genuine inclinations flow and solidify.

200

IT IS doubtful whether there is such a thing as impulsive or natural tolerance. Tolerance requires an effort of thought and self-control. And acts of kindness, too, are rarely without deliberateness and "thoughtfulness." Thus it seems that some artificiality, some posing and pretense, are inseparable from any act or attitude which involves a limitation of our appetites and selfishness.

We ought to beware of people who do not think it necessary to pretend that they are good and decent. Lack of hypocrisy in such things hints at a capacity for a most depraved ruthlessness.

201

THE reason that man is so fantastic a creature is that he is so superficial. His nobleness and vileness, his hatreds, loves and dedications are all of the surface. The sudden drastic transformations of which he is capable are due to the fact that his complex differentiation and the tensions which shape his attitudes are wholly surface phenomena.

202

WE PROBABLY have a greater love for those we support than those who support us. Our vanity carries more weight than our self-interest.

203

WHEN cowardice is made respectable, its followers are without number both from among the weak and the strong; it easily becomes a fashion.

204

THOSE who proclaim the brotherhood of men fight every war as if it were a civil war.

205

IT IS the inordinately selfish who need self-forgetting most, hence their proneness to passionate pursuits.

206

DEATH would have no terror were it to come a month from now, a week or even a day—but not tomorrow. For death has but one terror, that it has no tomorrow.

207

WE USUALLY yield to extremism not because we have no time to grow, but because we doubt that we are capable of growth.

208

SOME people are born to spend their lives catching up; and they are as a rule the passionate ones.

209

STUPIDITY is not always a mere want of intelligence. It can be a sort of corruption. It is doubtful whether the good of heart can be really stupid.

210

THE hardest thing to cope with is not selfishness or vanity or deceitfulness, but sheer stupidity. One needs the talents of an animal trainer to deal with the stupid.

211

WITH some people solitariness is an escape not from others but from themselves. For they see in the eyes of others only a reflection of themselves.

212

HUMILITY is not renunciation of pride but the substitution of one pride for another.

213

THE passionate are not as a rule culturally creative, but only they make history.

214

SELFLESSNESS is not infrequently a temporary regimen to which we submit in order to fortify and reinvigorate our selfishness.

215

TO KNOW a person's religion we need not listen to his profession of faith but must find his brand of intolerance.

216

ADD a few drops of venom to a half truth and you have an absolute truth.

217

OUR greatest pretenses are built up not to hide the evil and the ugly in us, but our emptiness. The hardest thing to hide is something that is not there.

218

THE real persuaders are our appetites, our fears and above all our vanity. The skillful propagandist stirs and coaches these internal persuaders.

219

MAN staggers through life yapped at by his reason, pulled and shoved by his appetites, whispered to by fears, beckoned by hopes. Small wonder that what he craves most is self-forgetting.

220

TO SPELL out the obvious is often to call it in question.

221

MEN weary as much of not doing the things they want to do as of doing the things they do not want to do.

222

YOU can discover what your enemy fears most by observing the means he uses to frighten you.

223

THERE is no loneliness greater than the loneliness of a failure. The failure is a stranger in his own house.

224

UNPREDICTABILITY, too, can become monotonous.

225

TAKE away hatred from some people, and you have men without faith.

226

IT REQUIRES a considerable degree of conceit to believe that we are loved. Only certain people can give us that conceit.

227

THE true prophet is not he who peers into the future but he who reads and reveals the present.

228

WHERE everything is possible miracles become commonplaces, but the familiar ceases to be self-evident.

229

WE LIKE to give but hate to lose. What affects us most is the gain and loss not in substance but in self-esteem.

230

IT IS not at all simple to understand the simple.

231

THE fear of becoming a "has been" keeps some people from becoming anything.

232

WE DO not really feel grateful toward those who make our dreams come true; they ruin our dreams.

233

WITHOUT a sense of proportion there can be neither good taste nor genuine intelligence, nor perhaps moral integrity.

234

SOME watch others to learn what to do, and some watch to learn what not to do.

235

THE best part of the art of living is to know how to grow old gracefully.

236

THERE is sublime thieving in all giving. Someone gives us all he has and we are his.

237

THE world leans on us. When we sag, the whole world seems to droop.

238

WE USUALLY see only the things we are looking for—so much so that we sometimes see them where they are not.

239

THE fervor which prompts us to renounce and destroy is not one of denial but of assertion. The iconoclast is often more idolatrous than the idol worshiper.

240

SOMETIMES the means we use to hide a thing serve only to advertise it.

241

RUDENESS is the weak man's imitation of strength.

242

WE FEEL free when we escape—even if it be but from the frying pan into the fire.

243

WE ARE unified both by hating in common and by being hated in common.

244

THOSE incapable of reverence are incapable of hatred. And those also of little faith are of little hatred.

245

HATRED often speaks the language of hope.

246

SELF-ESTEEM and self-contempt have specific odors; they can be smelled.

247

IT IS perhaps true that the hopeful cannot be tragic figures.

248

WE FIND it easy to exalt a person if by so doing we lower somewhat the already exalted.

249

LITTLE discomforts are borne less willingly than great sacrifices. For the former only worsen the present while the latter refute it.

250

IT IS always safe to assume that people are more subtle and less sensitive than they seem.

251

THERE is probably as much effort involved in being exquisitely wicked as in being exquisitely good.

252

THE more zeal the less heart. It seems that when we put all our heart into something we are left as it were heartless.

253

NOW that we know everything, we have also mastered the art of destroying the human spirit.

254

WE HAVE rudiments of reverence for the human body, but we consider as nothing the rape of the human mind.

255

FEAR and freedom are mutually exclusive.

256

THAT which serves as a substitute for self-seeking may eventually serve as its camouflage.

257

THE passion to get ahead is sometimes born of the fear lest we be left behind.

258

THERE is in imitation a passion for equality: to do as others do is to have blanket insurance that we shall not be left behind.

259

IT IS chiefly by their commonness that people are held in common.

260

PROPAGANDA does not deceive people; it merely helps them to deceive themselves.

261

MUCH of man's thinking is propaganda of his appetites.

262

A MAN by himself is in bad company.

263

SUFFERING cleanses only when it is free of resentment. Wholehearted contempt for our tormentors safeguards our soul from the mutilations of bitterness and hatred.

264

DISAPPOINTMENT is a sort of bankruptcy—the bankruptcy of a soul that expends too much in hope and expectation.

265

WISE living consists perhaps less in acquiring good habits than in acquiring as few habits as possible.

266

THE beginning of thought is in disagreement—not only with others but also with ourselves.

267

IT IS waiting that gives weight to time.

268

TO THE old, the new is usually bad news.

269

NAÏVETÉ in grownups is often charming; but when coupled with vanity it is indistinguishable from stupidity.

270

WIDESPREAD dissipation is the result rather than the cause of social decadence.

271

WASTING ourselves is sometimes a way of camouflaging our worthlessness: we hereby maintain the fiction that there was aught worth wasting.

272

IMITATION is often an act of separation from our insecure, hesitant self. There can be no religiosity, no enthusiasm and no heroism without imitation.

273

FAITH in ourselves, like every other faith, needs a chorus of consent.

274

NO ENDING is so final as a happy ending.

275

THE best reason for loving others is still that they love us.

276

A GREAT man's greatest good luck is to die at the right time.

277

WE HAVE a sense of power when we inflict pain—even if it be but on ourselves.

278

TO AGREE with us means much of the time to hate with us.

279

IT IS well to treasure the memories of past misfortunes; they constitute our bank of fortitude.

280

THE search for happiness is one of the chief sources of unhappiness.